Famous Buildings

WORLD
BOOK

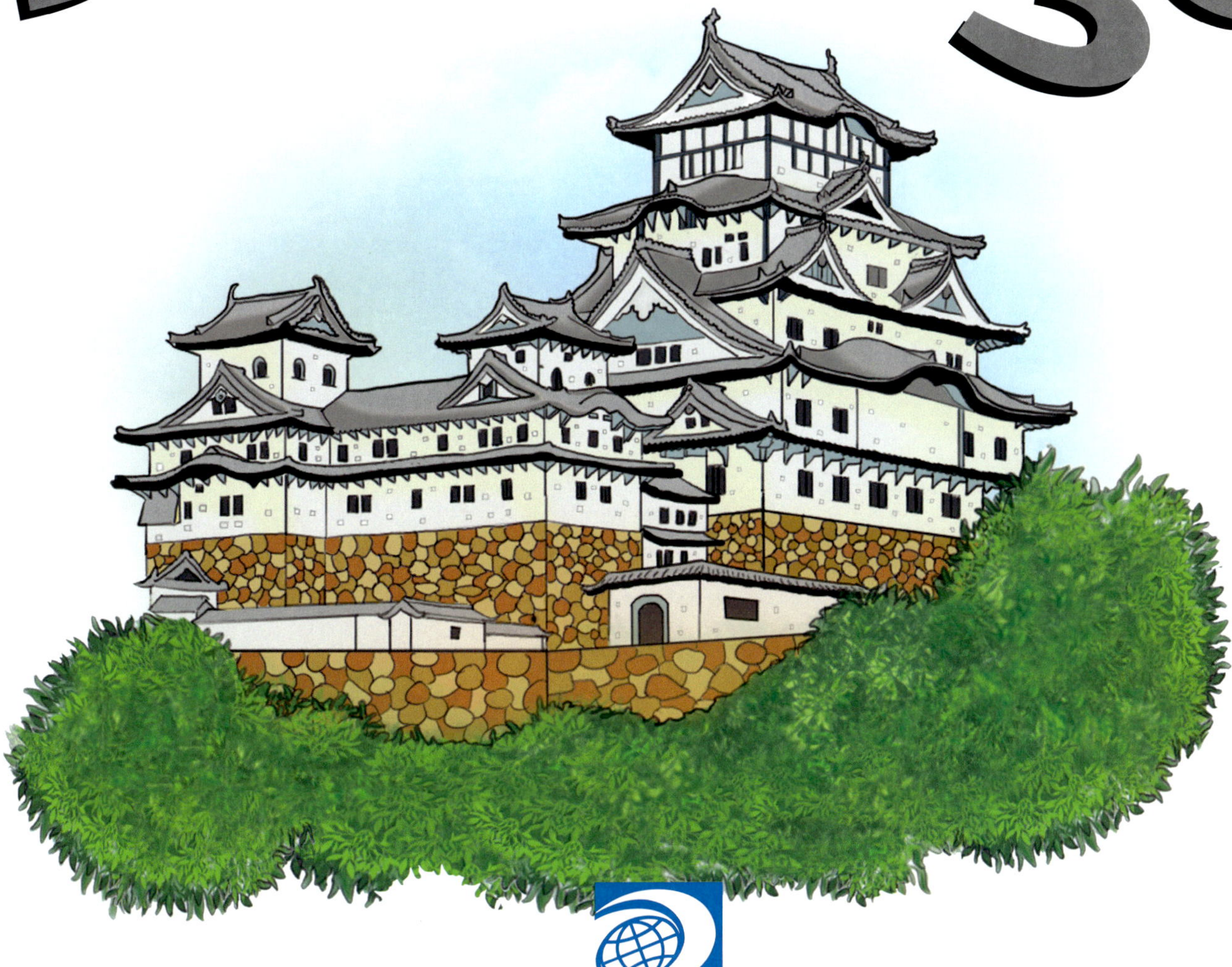

www.worldbook.com

World Book, Inc.
180 North LaSalle Street
Suite 900
Chicago, Illinois 60601
USA

For information about other World Book publications, visit our website at **www.worldbook.com** or call **1-800-WORLDBK (967-5325)**.

For information about sales to schools and libraries, call **1-800-975-3250 (United States); 1-800-837-5365 (Canada)**.

Library of Congress Cataloging-in-Publication Data for this volume has been applied for.

World Book's Learning Ladders
ISBN 978-0-7166-7945-5 (set, hc.)

Famous Buildings
ISBN 978-0-7166-7947-9 (hc.)

Also available as:
ISBN 978-0-7166-7957-8 (e-book)

Printed in China by Shenzhen Wing King Tong Paper Products Co, Ltd., Shenzhen, Guangdong
1st printing December 2017

Staff

Executive Committee
President: Jim O'Rourke
Vice President and Editor in Chief: Paul A. Kobasa
Vice President, Finance: Donald D. Keller
Vice President, Marketing: Jean Lin
Vice President, International Sales: Maksim Rutenberg
Vice President, Technology: Jason Dole
Director, Human Resources: Bev Ecker

Editorial
Director, New Print Publishing: Tom Evans
Senior Editor, New Print Publishing: Shawn Brennan
Writer: Echo Elise González
Director, Digital Product Content Development: Emily Kline
Manager, Indexing Services: David Pofelski
Manager, Contracts & Compliance (Rights & Permissions): Loranne K. Shields
Librarian: S. Thomas Richardson

Digital
Director, Digital Product Development: Erika Meller
Digital Product Manager: Jonathan Wills

Graphics and Design
Senior Art Director: Tom Evans
Coordinator, Design Development and Production: Brenda Tropinski
Senior Visual Communications Designer: Melanie J. Bender
Media Researcher: Rosalia Bledsoe

Manufacturing/Pre-Press
Manufacturing Manager: Anne Fritzinger
Proofreader: Nathalie Strassheim

Photographic credits: Cover: © Pisa Photography/Shutterstock; Eliedion (licensed under CC BY-SA 4.0): 7; Tony Hisgett (licensed under CC BY 2.0): 10; Gilles Mairet (licensed under CC BY-SA 3.0): 13; © Shutterstock: 4, 5, 6, 9, 11, 17, 20, 23, 26, 27; Jason Tong (licensed under CC BY 2.0): 19; The Christian Martyrs' Last Prayer (1883), oil on canvas by Jean-Léon Gérôme; Walters Art Museum: 9; Zigomar (licensed under CC BY-SA 3.0): 14.

Illustrators: WORLD BOOK illustrations by Quadrum Ltd

What's inside?

Architecture is the art of making buildings. Almost every culture has developed some form of architecture. This book tells you about different kinds of architecture and some famous buildings found around the world.

Burj Khalifa

Burj Khalifa *(BURJ kuh LEE fuh)* is one of the tallest buildings in the world. It stands 2,716 feet (828 meters) over the city of Dubai in the United Arab Emirates. *Burj* is an Arabic word meaning *tower*.

An 800-foot (244-meter) steel **spire** tops the building.

Burj Khalifa gleams with panels made of shiny, mirrorlike **glass**.

There are three **observation decks**—on the 124th, 125th, and 148th floors—in the Burj Khalifa. These decks are very high off the ground. You can see out for miles or kilometers through the floor-to-ceiling glass windows.

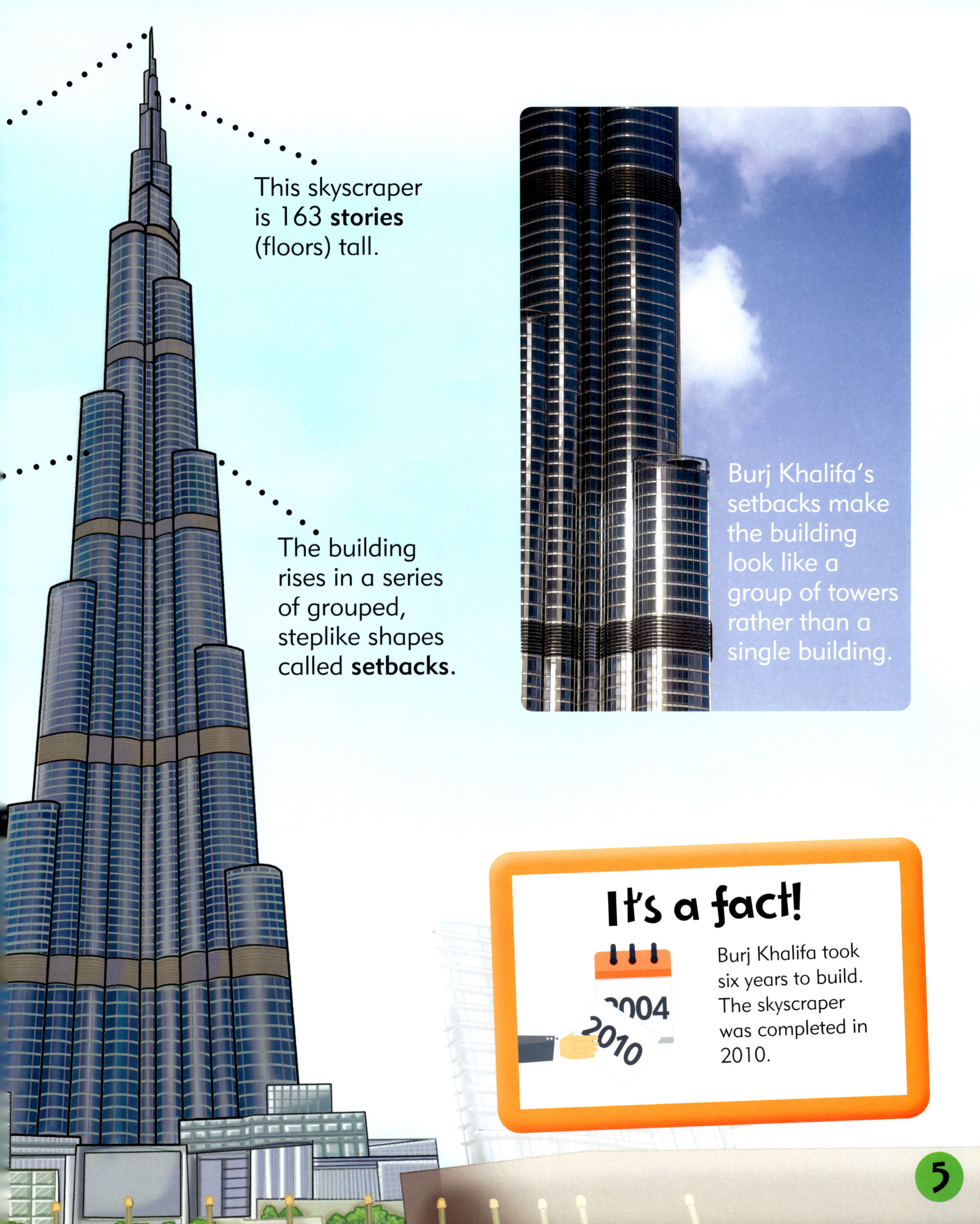

This skyscraper is 163 **stories** (floors) tall.

The building rises in a series of grouped, steplike shapes called **setbacks**.

Burj Khalifa's setbacks make the building look like a group of towers rather than a single building.

It's a fact!

Burj Khalifa took six years to build. The skyscraper was completed in 2010.

2004 2010

Château Frontenac

The Château Frontenac *(sha TOH FRON tuh nak)* is a famous hotel in the city of Quebec, Canada. *Château* is a French word that means *castle* or *large country house*. The hotel is on a cliff overlooking the St. Lawrence River. The hotel opened in 1893.

Dormer windows are cut through the roof of a building.

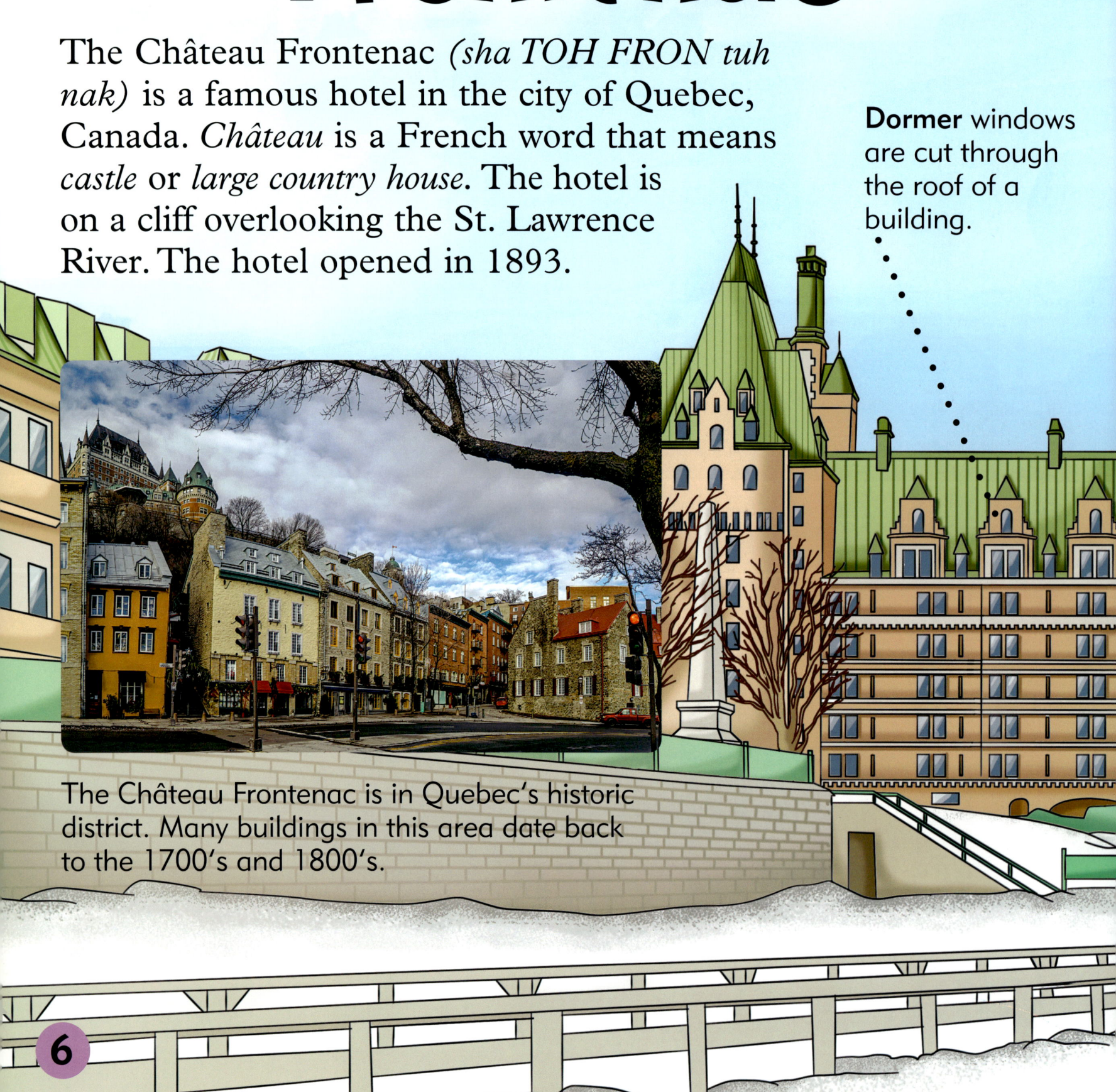

The Château Frontenac is in Quebec's historic district. Many buildings in this area date back to the 1700's and 1800's.

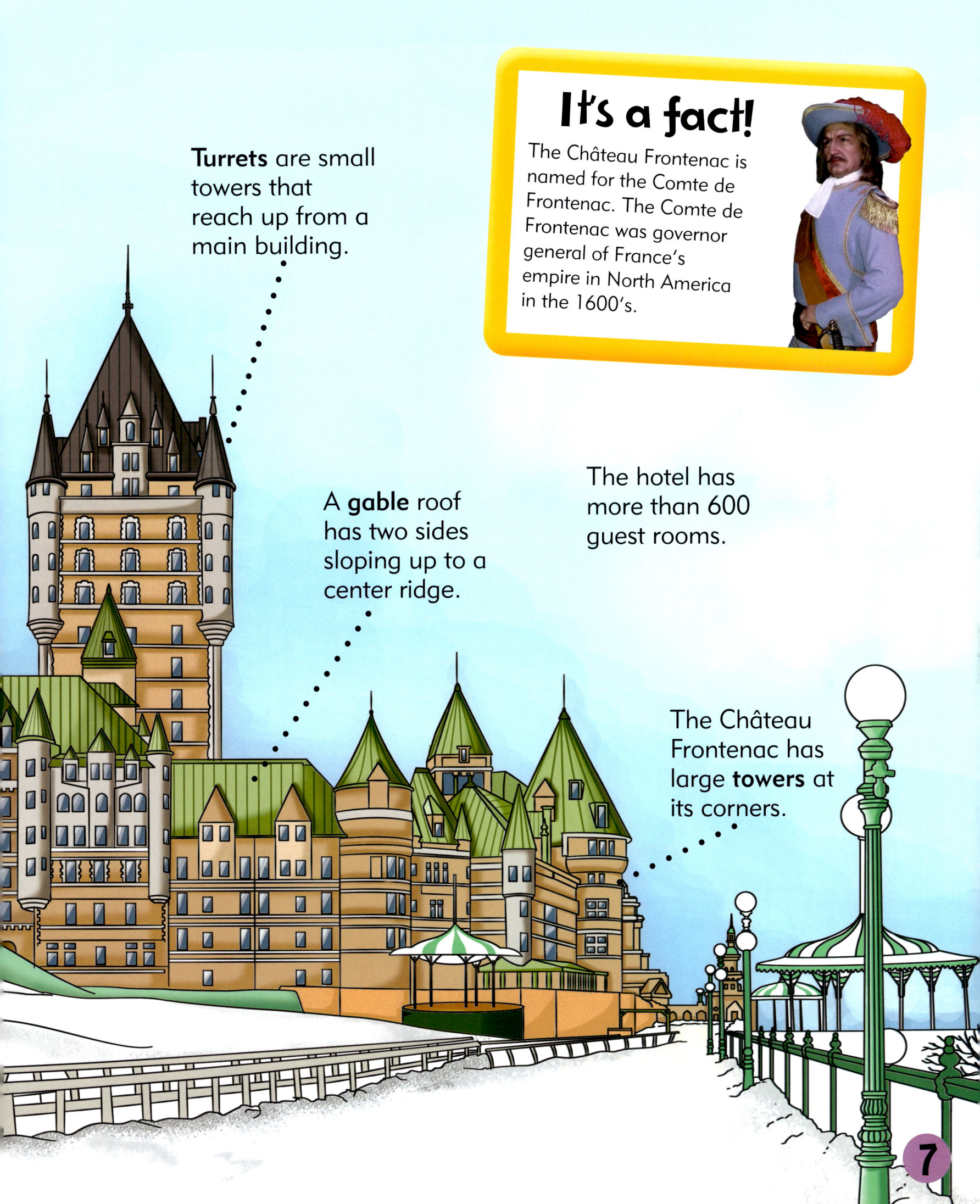

Turrets are small towers that reach up from a main building.

A gable roof has two sides sloping up to a center ridge.

The hotel has more than 600 guest rooms.

The Château Frontenac has large towers at its corners.

Colosseum

The Colosseum *(kol uh SEE uhm)* is a large outdoor theater in Rome, Italy. It is one of the finest examples of the architecture of ancient Rome. The theater is almost 2,000 years old. Today, the Colosseum is a historical landmark.

The four-story **theater** once seated up to 50,000 people.

The Colosseum is made of brick and concrete. Stone covers the **exterior.**

The oval building has about 80 **entrances** and hundreds of **arches.**

Passages and rooms below the Colosseum floor helped warriors and animals move back and forth during a live event.

The Colosseum was once used for fights between trained warriors called **gladiators** and battles between men and wild animals. Other shows included battles between ships. The floor of the Colosseum would be flooded with water for these pretend battles.

Empire State Building

The Empire State Building is one of the most famous landmarks in New York City in the United States. It measures 1,250 feet (381 meters) tall from the sidewalk to the roof. The skyscraper is named for the state of New York, which is sometimes called the *Empire State*. The building was finished in 1931.

The Empire State Building is 102 **stories** tall. It was the tallest building in the world for many years.

The Empire State Building uses a style called **Art Deco** that was popular in the 1930's. Art Deco buildings have geometric shapes and smooth lines.

The Empire State building is topped by a metal **spire** that is more than 200 feet (61 meters) tall.

The building rises in a series of **setbacks** to a narrow **tower.**

Panels of a light colored rock called **limestone** and a metal mixture cover the skyscraper's steel framework.

The tower lights in the Empire State Building change color to help celebrate many different events. A green light shines on Earth Day, a day in April which celebrates our planet.

It's a fact!

In the 1933 monster movie *King Kong,* the giant ape named Kong climbs to the top of the Empire State Building and battles fighter planes.

Great Mosque of Djénné

The Great Mosque of Djénné *(jeh NAY)* is the largest mud brick building on Earth. It stands in the city of Djénné in Mali, Africa. A mosque *(mosk)* is a religious building used for Muslim worship. The Great Mosque has been rebuilt three times. The building we see today was built in 1907.

Most mosques have one or more prayer towers called **minarets**. Some minarets have a small **spire** at the top.

Each year, the people of Djénné hold a festival where they cover the cracks in the Great Mosque with fresh layers of **mud**.

The mosque's roof has some small holes that let fresh air into the building. These holes are partly covered by **terra-cotta** (claylike) lids.

Beams of palm wood stick out from the sides of the building.

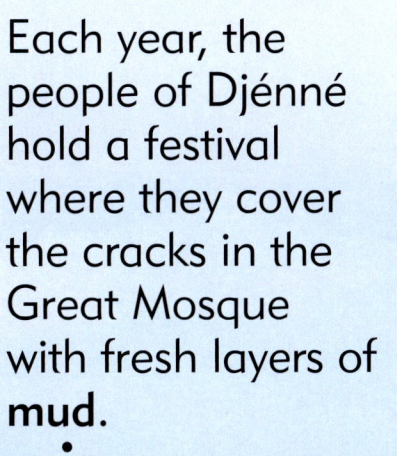

It's a fact!

The mosque is built from bricks made of mud and straw. The bricks are left to dry in the sun before they are stacked to form the building's walls.

Himeji Castle

Himeji *(hee MAY jee)* Castle is one of the most beautiful buildings in Japan. It stands across the tops of two hills on southern Honshu Island. It was first built in 1346, but some of the first buildings were ruined. Today, people work to keep the castle in good shape for the many visitors who travel to see it.

Small **openings** in the castle walls were once used for throwing stones and other objects at attackers.

The castle **complex** (group of buildings and passages) has over 80 buildings, gates, and walls. There are many confusing pathways that connect these structures. Three moats (waterways) once surrounded the castle. Having so many buildings and moats in the complex helped to protect the main castle from invaders.

The castle's outer walls are made of wood and covered with **plaster**.

It's a fact!

The castle's nickname is *Shirasagi-jo*, which means *white heron castle*. It got this nickname from the white color of its outer walls and the curved shape of the roof, which looks like the wings of a bird called a heron.

The main **keep** (tower) is five stories tall.

Palace of Heavenly Purity

The Palace of Heavenly Purity was once the home of many ancient Chinese emperors. It was originally built in the 1400's. Today, it stands in the Forbidden City, a historic walled area in Beijing, China's capital. The Palace of Heavenly Purity is the largest building in the Forbidden City.

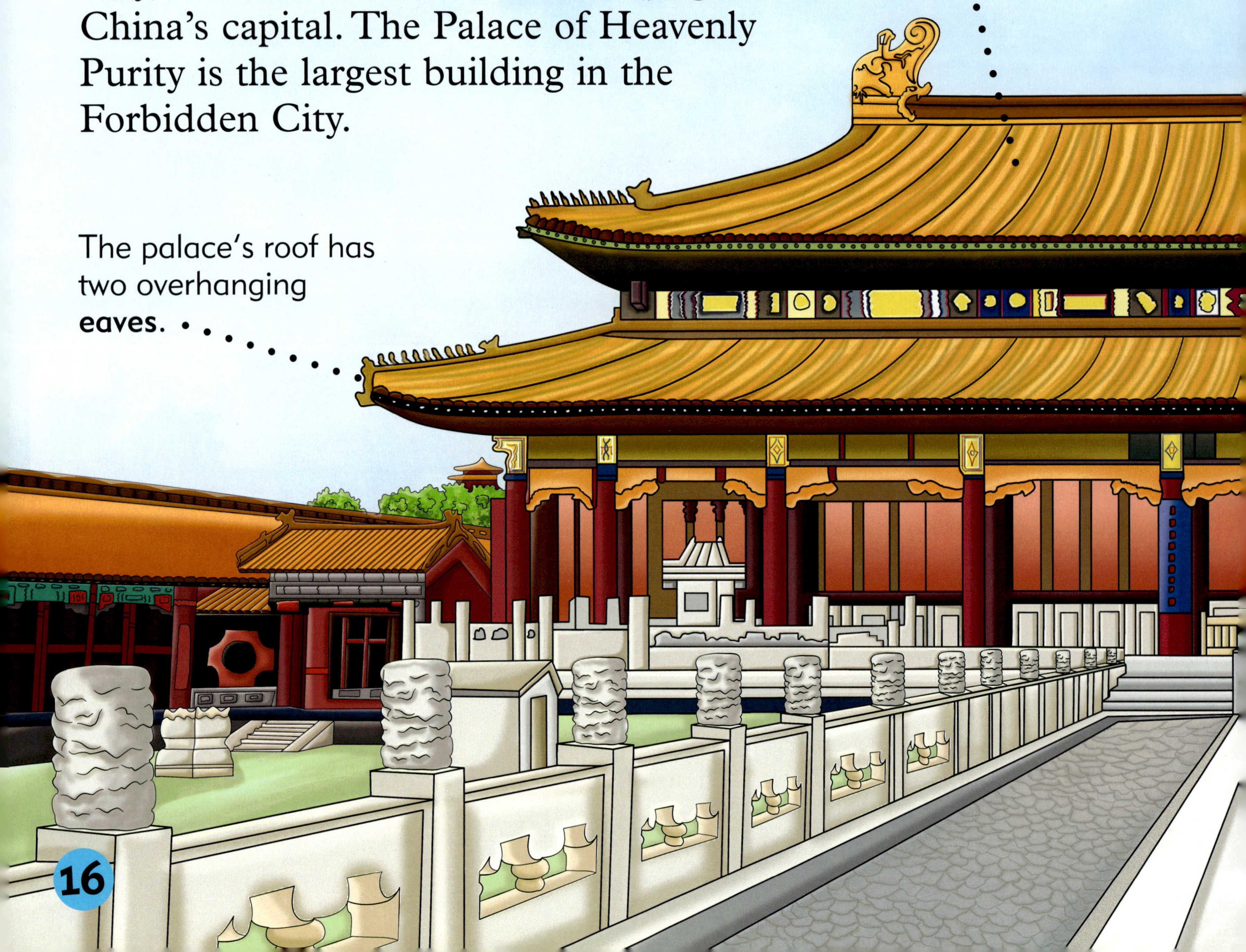

The **roof** is made from yellow **tiles**. Yellow is a symbol for the earth and the emperor.

The palace's roof has two overhanging **eaves**.

The Palace of Heavenly Purity was rebuilt after it was destroyed by a fire in the 1700's.

The throne room is inside the Palace of Heavenly Purity. In this room, emperors once signed important papers and held special meetings and ceremonies. The room is decorated with mirrors, Chinese phrases, and drawings.

Ten red **columns** stand at the front of the palace. Chinese people think of red as the color of luck and happiness.

A stone **walkway** leads to the front of the palace.

17

Sydney Opera House

The Sydney Opera House is one of the most famous buildings in Australia. It stands in the city of Sydney. The building has a main concert hall and some smaller theaters where musicians and actors put on shows for audiences. There are other performance areas, too.

The building's **forecourt** is used as an outdoor performance space.

The building overlooks Sydney Harbour. A **harbor** is an area of deep water that is protected from wind and waves because of the shape of the land around it.

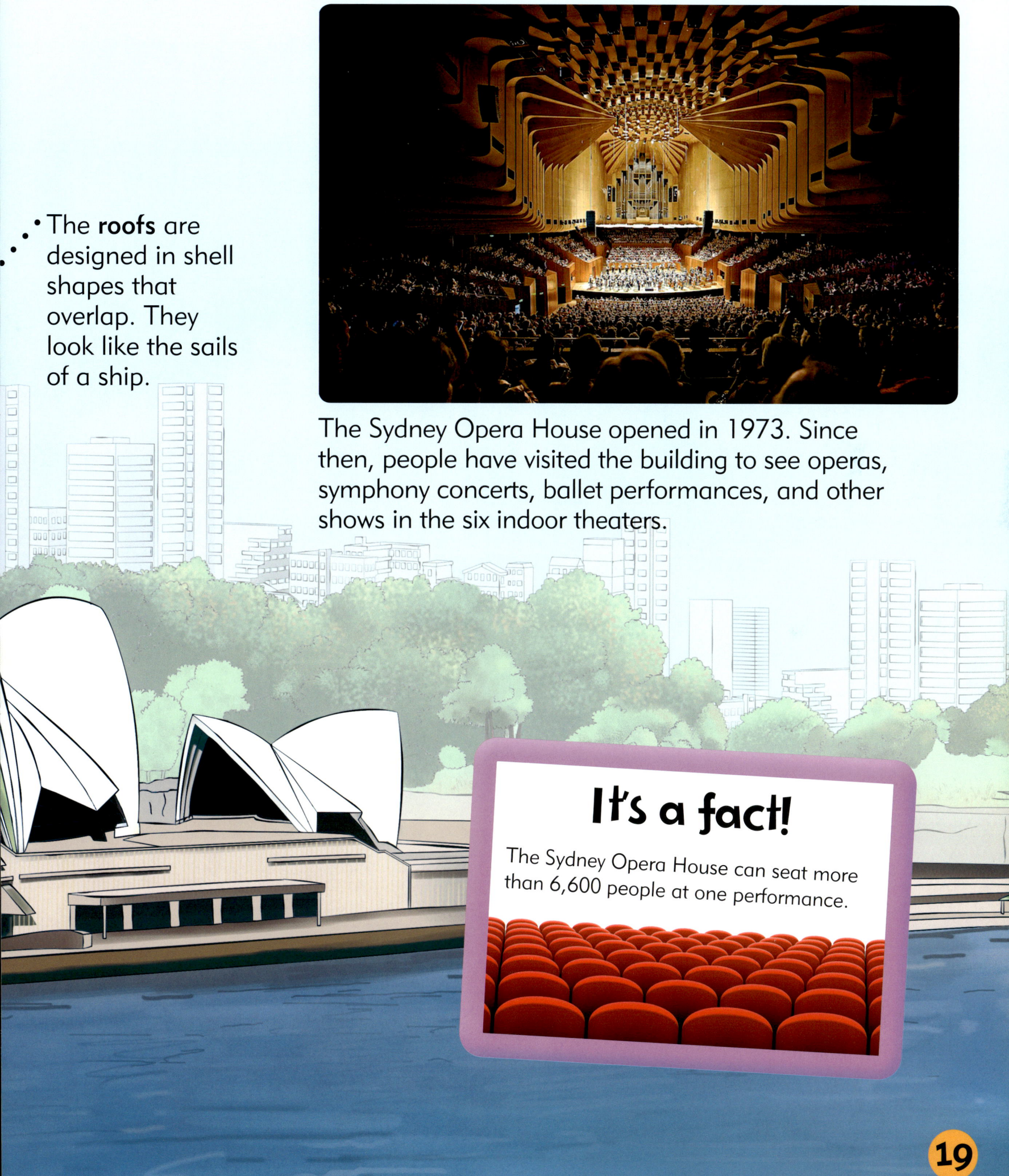

The **roofs** are designed in shell shapes that overlap. They look like the sails of a ship.

The Sydney Opera House opened in 1973. Since then, people have visited the building to see operas, symphony concerts, ballet performances, and other shows in the six indoor theaters.

It's a fact!

The Sydney Opera House can seat more than 6,600 people at one performance.

Taj Mahal

The Taj Mahal *(TAHJ muh HAHL)* is a beautiful tomb (burial place) in Agra in northern India. An Indian ruler named Shah Jahan built the tomb in memory of his wife Mumtaz Mahal. It took 20,000 workers 20 years to build the Taj Mahal. It was completed in 1650. Shah Jahan was later buried there as well.

A round **dome** rises over the center of the square building.

The walls are made of white **marble,** a type of stone.

Beautiful **gardens** and **fountains** lead the way up to the Taj Mahal's main entrance.

Inside the tomb, visitors can see the two monuments to the dead couple through a beautiful white carved screen.

Four **minarets** are around the building.

The building stands on a **platform** of red sandstone rock.

Windsor Castle

Windsor Castle is where the British queen or king and members of her or his family live when they are not at Buckingham Palace in London, England. The queen's or king's family is called the royal family.

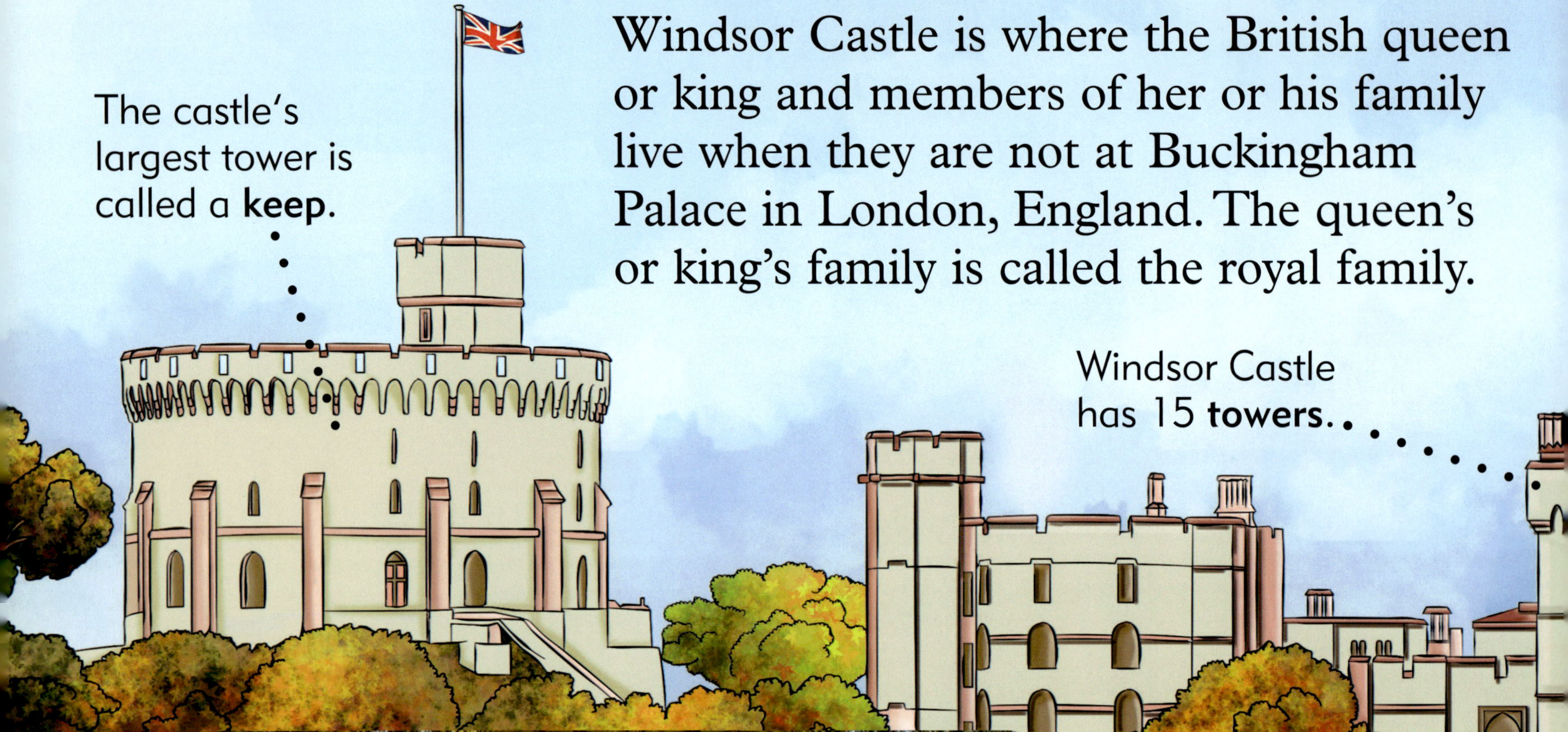

The castle's largest tower is called a **keep**.

Windsor Castle has 15 **towers**.

One of the most famous parts of Windsor Castle is St. George's Chapel. A **chapel** is a type of church. St. George's Chapel took 50 years to build. It has a huge ceiling and stained glass windows.

22

Windsor Castle stands in the Home Park, a beautiful royal **park.** Only the royal family and their guests can go into the park.

It's a fact!

Windsor Castle has been the home to British royalty for almost 1,000 years. Kings and queens have added rooms to the castle over time. Today, Windsor Castle has about 1,000 rooms.

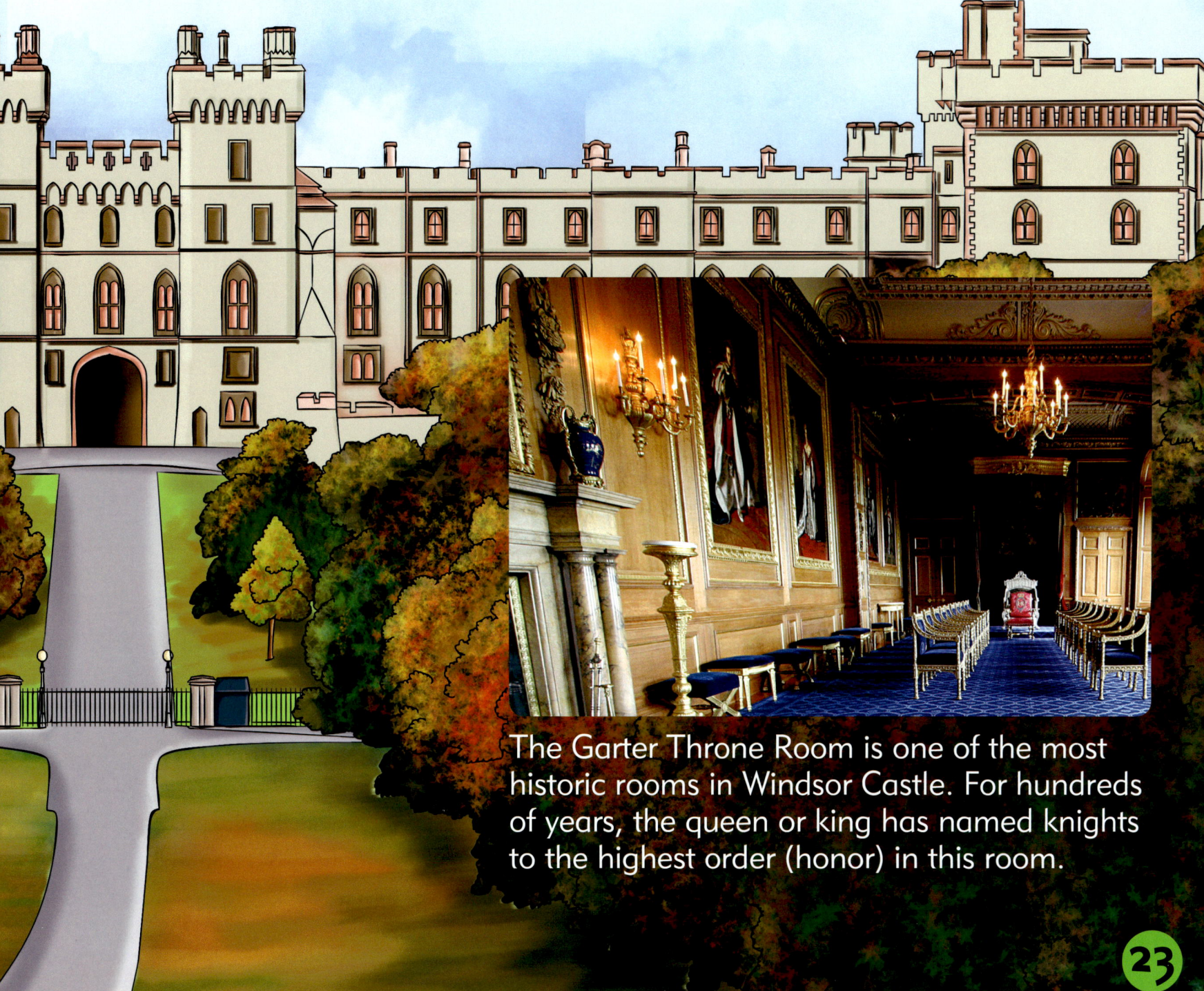

The Garter Throne Room is one of the most historic rooms in Windsor Castle. For hundreds of years, the queen or king has named knights to the highest order (honor) in this room.

Around the world

Amazing buildings can be found around the world. Some were built for people to live or work in. Others are where people go to worship or enjoy music or other entertainments.

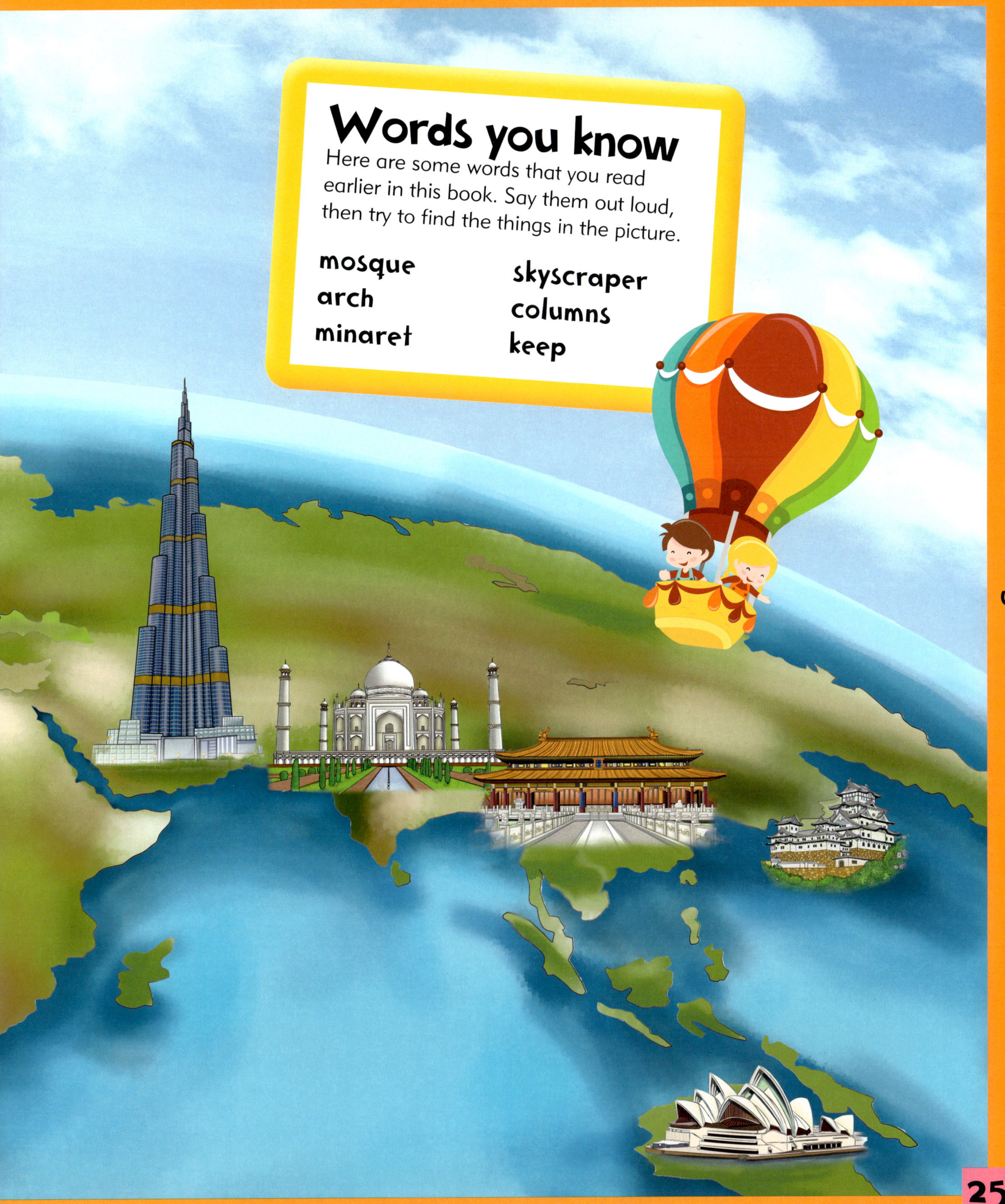

Words you know

Here are some words that you read earlier in this book. Say them out loud, then try to find the things in the picture.

mosque
arch
minaret

skyscraper
columns
keep

Which building is the tallest?

25

Did you know?

The Great Pyramid stands in Giza *(GEE zuh)*, Egypt. It was built about 4,500 years ago as the tomb for the ruler Khufu *(KOO foo)*.

Angkor Wat *(ANG kohr wot)* is an old temple in Cambodia. Its stone walls are decorated with carvings.

The Cathedral of Notre Dame *(noh truh DAHM)* in Paris, France, is a famous building with many pointed arches.

The Parthenon (PAHR thuh non) is a temple overlooking the city of Athens, Greece. It was built nearly 2,500 years ago.

Machu Picchu (MAH choo PEEK choo) stands high in the mountains of Peru. It was probably once the home of the ancient Incan royal family.

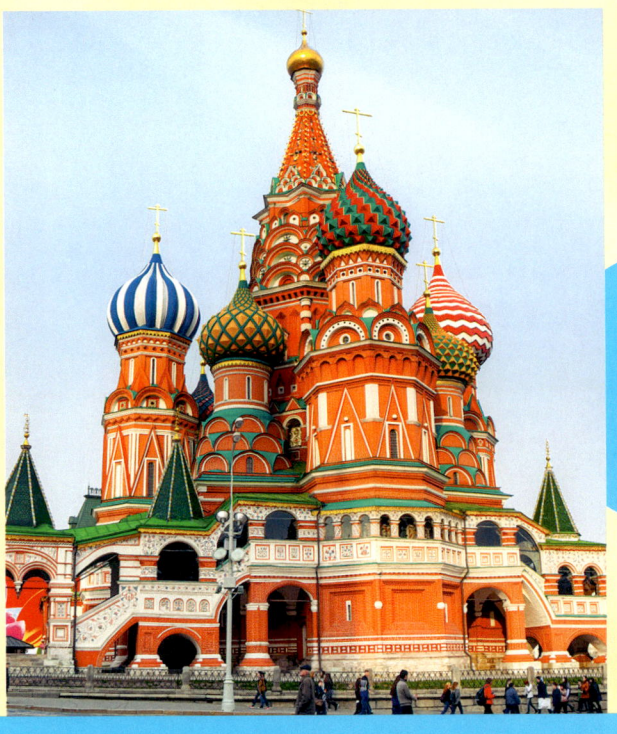

St. Basil's Cathedral in Moscow, Russia, has many bright, colorful domes.

Puzzles

Close-up!

We've zoomed in on three different buildings. Can you figure out which buildings you are looking at?

1

2

3

Double trouble!

These two pictures are not exactly the same. What are five things in picture b that are different from picture a?

a

b

Answers on page 32.

Match up!

Match each building name on the left with its picture on the right.

a

1. Taj Mahal

b

2. Windsor Castle

c

3. Château Frontenac

d

4. Colosseum

5. Himeji Castle

e

6. Empire State Building

f

Answers on page 32.

True or false

Can you figure out which of these statements are true? Go to the page numbers given to help you find the answers.

3 The Château Frontenac is in Paris, France.
Go to page 6.

1 The Empire State Building uses a style called Art Deco.
Go to page 10.

4 The Taj Mahal is a library in India.
Go to page 20.

2 Pretend naval battles were sometimes held in the Colosseum.
Go to page 9.

5 Windsor Castle is in an amusement park.
Go to page 23.

Answers on page 32.

Find out more

Books

Building Structures and Towers by Tammy Enz (Heinemann-Raintree, 2017)
This volume uses engaging nonfiction text and hands-on projects to help young readers explore real-life structure- and tower-engineering projects, including the science behind how these buildings are planned and built.

How a Skyscraper Is Built by Therese Shea (Gareth Stevens, 2016)
Readers will see the construction of skyscrapers for themselves through vivid photographs and diagrams of a building on its way from its beginning on an empty lot to a monster skyscraper touching the skies.

Skyscrapers by Virginia Loh-Hagan (Cherry Lake, 2017)
This volume examines the engineering concepts that make these awe-inspiring structures possible. Sidebars encourage readers to engage in the material by asking deeper questions or conducting individual research. Includes activities, full-color photos, a glossary, and a listing of additional resources.

Skyscrapers by Libby Romero (National Geographic Society, 2017)
Learn all about the world's most amazing skyscrapers—from the first, to the tallest, to how they're built, and everything in between—in this National Geographic Kids book.

Websites

Ancient Greece
http://www.ancientgreece.com/s/Art/
 Explore the history of art and architecture in the ancient Greek world.

The Great Buildings Collection
http://www.greatbuildings.com/
ArchitectureWeek's Great Buildings website features illustrations of more than 1,000 buildings from around the world.

History for Kids: Ancient and Medieval Architecture
http://quatr.us/architecture/
Find out more about the history of ancient and medieval architecture on this student-friendly website.

Skyscraper Page
http://skyscraperpage.com/
This website provides information on skyscrapers and buildings from around the world.

Answers

Puzzles

from pages 28 and 29

Close-up!
1. Colosseum
2. Château Frontenac
3. Taj Mahal

Double trouble!
In picture b, the girl's hat is tipped in the opposite direction, she is holding her cell phone vertically instead of horizontally, the tree in front of the black building moved right, the ferry boat changed places with the sailboat, and one of the triangular roofs on the Sydney Opera House is missing.

Match up!

1. f	2. a	3. e
4. b	5. d	6. c

True or false

from page 30

1. true	4. false
2. true	5. false
3. false	

Index